RANDY ORTON

by Michael Sandler

Consultant: Eric Cohen
Professional Wrestling Guide for About.com
prowrestling.about.com

BEARPORT
PUBLISHING

New York, New York

Credits

Cover and Title Page, © Bob Levey/WireImage/Getty Images; ; TOC, © Bob Levey/WireImage/Getty Images; 4, © Matt Roberts-ZUMA Press/Alamy; 5TL, © Titomedia.com/Splash News/Newscom; 5TM, © Anna Ker/WP/Panoramic/ZUMA Press/Newscom; 5TR, © Matt Roberts-ZUMA Press/Newscom; 5BR, © Don Arnold/WireImage/Getty Images; 6, © Bob Levey/WireImage/Getty Images; 7, © World Wrestling Entertainment/ZUMA Press/Newscom; 8L, © Graham Whitby/Globe Photos/ZUMA Press/Newscom; 8R, © Michael Abramson/Liaison/Getty Images; 9, © Walter Iooss Jr./Sports Illustrated/Getty Images; 10, © Sid Hastings; 11, ©Brownie Harris/Corbis; 13, © Tom 'Mo' Moschella/Icon SMI/ZUMA Press; 14, © Carrie Devorah/WENN/Newscom; 15, © Djamilla Rosa Cochran/WireImage/Getty Images; 16, © Tom 'Mo' Moschella/Icon SMI/ZUMA Press; 17, © Panoramic/ZUMA Press/Newscom; 18, © Djamilla Rosa Cochran/WireImage/Getty Images; 18, © John Barrett/Globe Photos/ZUMA Press/Newscom; 19, © Milan Ryba/Globe Photos/ZUMA Press/Newscom; 20, © Bob Levey/WireImage/Getty Images; 21, © Rob Loud/Getty Images; 22T, © Carrie Devorah/WENN/Newscom; 22B, © Panoramic/ZUMA Press/Newscom.

Publisher: Kenn Goin
Senior Editor: Lisa Wiseman
Creative Director: Spencer Brinker
Photo Researcher: We Research Pictures, LLC
Design: Debrah Kaiser

Library of Congress Cataloging-in-Publication Data

Sandler, Michael, 1965-
  Randy Orton / by Michael Sandler ; consultant, Eric Cohen.
     p. cm. — (Wrestling's tough guys)
  Includes bibliographical references and index.
  ISBN 978-1-61772-572-2 (library binding) — ISBN 1-61772-572-2 (library binding)
  1. Orton, Randy—Juvenile literature. 2. Wrestlers—United States—Biography—Juvenile literature. I. Cohen, Eric. II. Title.
  GV1196.O77S26 2013
  796.812092—dc23
  [B]

                         2012007275

For more information, write to Bearport Publishing Company, Inc., 45 West 21st Street, Suite 3B, New York, New York 10010. Printed in the United States of America.

10 9 8 7 6 5 4 3 2 1

Contents

Ready to Rumble

Despite winning just about every **WWE title**, Randy Orton had never survived a Royal Rumble. Now he was about to wrestle in the 2009 match. Would things turn out differently for him this time?

Randy Orton

As the 2009 Royal Rumble began, WWE superstars, one by one, leaped into the ring at 90-second **intervals**. Rey Mysterio, the tiny former **World Heavyweight Champion**, was first. Then came John Morrison, Carlito, MVP, The Great Khali, Vladimir Kozlov, and Triple H. Soon it was Randy's turn. Slipping through the ropes, the 6 feet 5 (1.96 m), 235-pound (107-kg) wrestler launched himself at Triple H and began pounding him on the head. Suddenly, three other wrestlers began hammering Randy. Winning this rumble wasn't going to be easy!

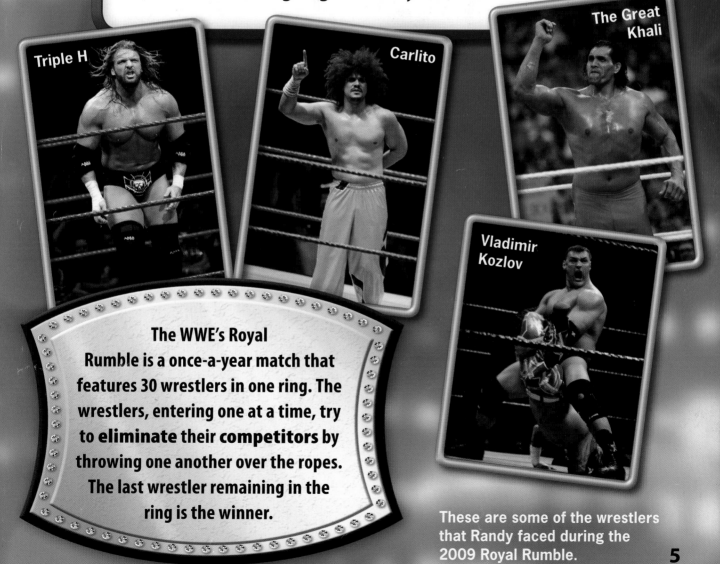

Triple H

Carlito

The Great Khali

Vladimir Kozlov

The WWE's Royal Rumble is a once-a-year match that features 30 wrestlers in one ring. The wrestlers, entering one at a time, try to **eliminate** their **competitors** by throwing one another over the ropes. The last wrestler remaining in the ring is the winner.

These are some of the wrestlers that Randy faced during the 2009 Royal Rumble.

Last Man Standing

As the mad battle continued, more wrestlers piled into the ring. Bodies flew everywhere. One by one, wrestlers were eliminated. Soon there were just six left—Randy, Triple H, Big Show, Undertaker, Cody Rhodes, and Ted DiBiase.

Randy (right) in the ring with Triple H (left) during another match in 2009

Randy knew he had to do everything he could to win the match. With all his power, he knocked Big Show out of the rumble with a rattling RKO. As Big Show left the ring, he took Undertaker with him. Now just four wrestlers remained. Then Triple H flipped two of them out of the ring, leaving only him and Randy. In a flash, Randy was on Triple H, grabbing and tossing him over the top rope. Randy was the last man standing. He had won the Royal Rumble!

Randy celebrates after winning the 2009 Royal Rumble.

The RKO is Randy's favorite finishing move. The letters stand for the initials in Randy's full name—Randal Keith Orton. To perform the RKO, Randy grabs his opponent by the neck and slams him to the mat with lightning speed.

Family Tree

Long before the Royal Rumble, Randy was used to being surrounded by wrestlers. As a child growing up in St. Louis, Missouri, his house was often full of wrestlers. Sometimes Randy would walk into the kitchen and see "Rowdy" Roddy Piper or Andre the Giant sitting at the table.

Randy grew up surrounded by superstar wrestlers such as "Rowdy" Roddy Piper (left) and Andre the Giant (right).

The wrestlers were friends of Randy's father, a wrestling star known as "Cowboy" Bob Orton. Wrestling ran in his family. His grandfather, Bob Orton, Sr., was also a wrestler, and so was one of his uncles.

"Cowboy" Bob Orton (second from left) in the ring before the first WrestleMania

Randy was around five years old when he watched his father at the very first WrestleMania, the most important WWE wrestling event of the year.

Don't Be a Wrestler

Even though Randy's family was full of wrestlers, his parents tried to discourage him from becoming a pro wrestler himself. Wrestling was tough, they told him. Wrestlers got hurt. They traveled too much. "Cowboy" Bob was away from home for months at a time. He rarely had time to spend with his family.

Hazelwood Central High School in Missouri

Randy had wrestled in high school at Hazelwood Central High School. He had been very good, winning most of his senior-year matches.

Randy listened to his parents and decided to try other careers first. After high school, he signed up to become a Marine. He served for less than two years. Then he left the military and went back to St. Louis. For a while, he worked in a gas station and lived in his parents' basement.

The Marine Corps is one of the four main branches of the U.S. military. Marines are trained to fight on land and at sea.

Becoming a Pro Wrestler

One night, while watching wrestling on TV, 19-year-old Randy realized that being a wrestler was what he really wanted to do. He told his father how he felt. Shortly after, Randy's father took him to a WWE match and introduced him to some officials. They agreed to give Randy a chance to try out as a wrestler.

Randy impressed the officials during his tryout. By 2001, the WWE had sent him to train and wrestle at Ohio Valley Wrestling, its training school in Louisville, Kentucky. There, he practiced with other young wrestlers such as future WWE champion John Cena.

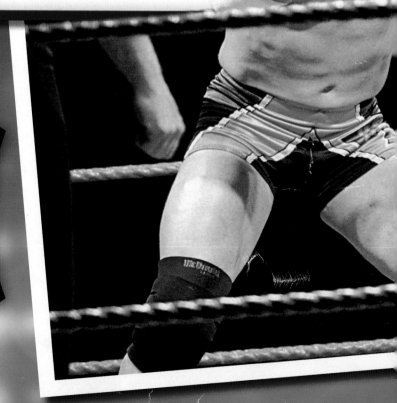

Randy's first televised WWE match was against Bob Holly in 2002. Randy slammed Bob to the canvas within ten seconds. Later Randy ended the match with an **Oklahoma Side Roll** for the **pin**.

Bob Holly (left) during a match against CM Punk (right)

The Legend Killer

Even as a brand-new WWE wrestler, Randy was extremely confident. He insulted older, more famous wrestlers outside the ring, and then went on to beat them in the ring. As a result, he decided to go by the name "**Legend** Killer," promising to defeat every wrestling legend who ever lived.

andy (right) puts
hawn Michaels (left)
nto a headlock.

Living up to his name, Randy took on the WWE's all-time greats, one by one. Randy challenged Shawn Michaels, Dusty Rhodes, Sgt. Slaughter, Harley Race, and Mick Foley. He earned a **reputation** as the WWE's most **arrogant** and ferocious young wrestler. These qualities also earned him a shot at the World Heavyweight Championship after barely two years as a WWE pro.

Randy won his first championship in the WWE, The Intercontinental Championship, in 2003. He held the title for seven months, successfully defending it against several other wrestlers, including Mick Foley.

Randy (left) battles Mick Foley (right) in 2004.

The Youngest Champion

Randy's shot at the World Heavyweight Championship title arrived in August 2004 against Chris Benoit, an extremely skilled wrestler. Early in the year, Chris had won the Royal Rumble. Then, a few months later, he took the World Heavyweight Championship by crushing WWE powerhouses Triple H and Shawn Michaels in a **Triple Threat Match**.

Chris Benoit jumps off the top rope during a match.

Randy respected no one, but he appreciated Chris's power. Early on in the match, the champion **pummeled** Randy. Chris was on his way to a win. Then Randy shocked Chris with his finishing move, the RKO. The powerhouse move knocked out Chris. Randy was now the World Heavyweight Champion!

Randy was just 24 years old when he defeated Chris Benoit. He became the youngest World Heavyweight Champion in WWE history. He lost the title later on in 2004. However, in 2011, he got it back with a big win over Canadian superstar Christian.

Randy holds up the World Heavyweight Championship belt after defeating Christian in 2011.

Victories for the Viper

After Randy's huge win over Chris Benoit, more titles followed. In 2006, he formed the Rated-RKO **tag team** with fellow WWE superstar Edge. Within months, Randy and Edge had grabbed the World Tag Team Championship from Ric Flair and "Rowdy" Roddy Piper. Then, in a one-on-one match the following year, Randy beat **rival** Triple H for the **WWE Championship**.

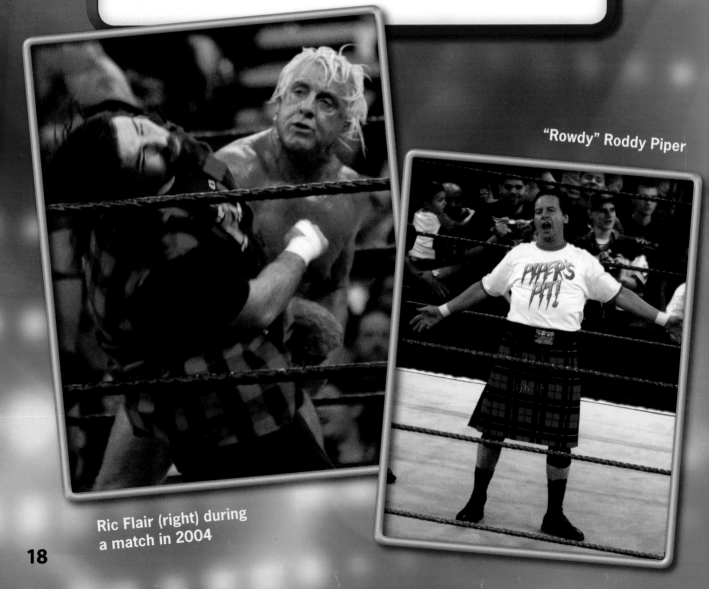

"Rowdy" Roddy Piper

Ric Flair (right) during a match in 2004

Throughout the years, Randy has continued to keep up his "legend-killing" ways. Sometimes he wins, such as when he destroyed Ric Flair in a 2004 **Steel Cage Match**, tossing the older wrestler around like a doll. Sometimes he loses—Undertaker, in 2005, and Hulk Hogan, in 2006, proved too tough for Randy. However, there is no wrestler Randy has ever feared to challenge.

Here, Undertaker puts Randy in a headlock.

"Legend Killer" is not the only name that Randy has used. He also goes by several others, including "The Viper." He is called this because he's as quick and deadly as the fearsome snake.

Living Legend

For Randy, reaching wrestling's highest level hasn't been easy. Just as his parents warned, he has been injured many times, and the life of a pro wrestler means constant training and travel. Now a father himself, Randy knows how hard it is to find time to spend with his family.

Randy makes his way into a ring.

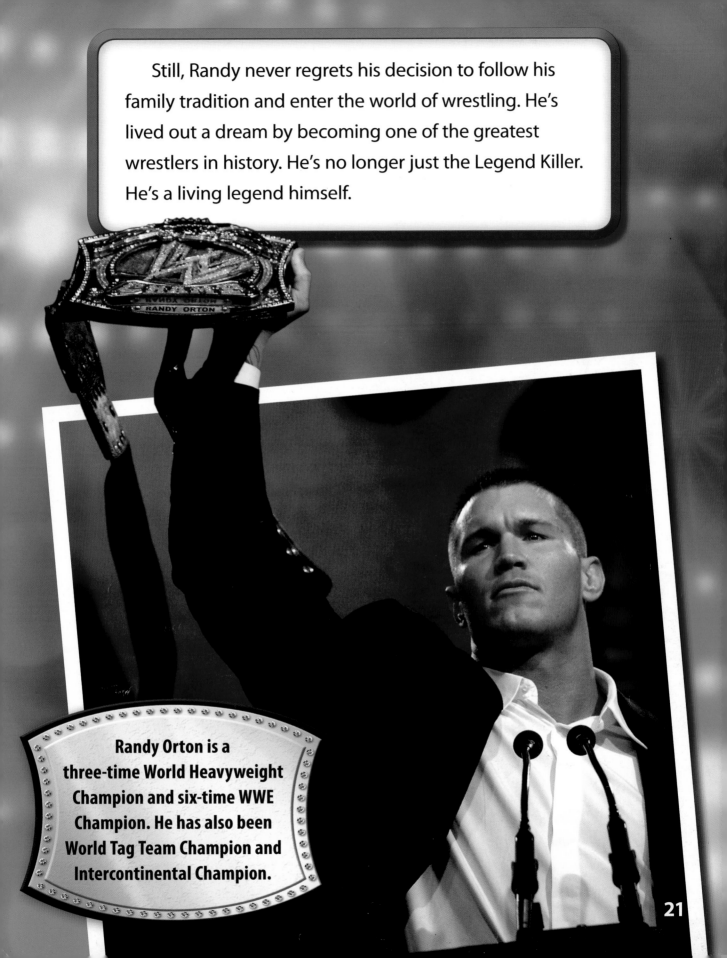

Still, Randy never regrets his decision to follow his family tradition and enter the world of wrestling. He's lived out a dream by becoming one of the greatest wrestlers in history. He's no longer just the Legend Killer. He's a living legend himself.

Randy Orton is a three-time World Heavyweight Champion and six-time WWE Champion. He has also been World Tag Team Champion and Intercontinental Champion.

The Randy Orton File

Stats:

Born:	April 1, 1980, Knoxville, Tennessee
Height:	6′ 5″ (1.96 m)
Weight:	235 pounds (107 kg)
Greatest moves:	RKO, Punt, Elevated DDT

Fun Facts:

- Randy has what doctors call "hypermobile" shoulders. This means his shoulders are so flexible that he can bend his arms farther back from his shoulders than most people are able to.

- In his spare time, Randy loves going to monster truck rallies.

- Randy broke his collarbone in the ring during a 2007 match against Triple H.

Randy (left) gets ready to hit WWE wrestler Sheamus (right).

Glossary

arrogant (A-ruh-guhnt) overly confident, too proud of oneself

competitors (kuhm-PET-i-turz) people who take part in a contest or sporting event

eliminate (uh-LIM-*uh*-nate) to remove from competition

intervals (IN-tur-vuhlz) time periods between two events

legend (LEJ-uhnd) a person who becomes very famous for a talent or an action

Oklahoma Side Roll (*oh*-kluh-HOH-muh SIDE ROHL) a move in which a wrestler rolls over an opponent who is on his or her knees, grabs the opponent by one arm and one leg, and turns him or her over, pressing his or her shoulders to the mat for the pin

pin (PIN) when a wrestler ends a match by holding his or her opponent's shoulders down on the floor for a count of three

pummeled (PUM-uhld) to strike or hit repeatedly

reputation (*rep*-yuh-TAY-shuhn) the opinion that most people have about a person

rival (RYE-vuhl) the main person one is competing against

Steel Cage Match (STEEL KAYJ MACH) a wrestling event that takes place within an enclosed metal cage; one of the ways to win the match is to escape the cage

tag team (TAG TEEM) a team of two or more wrestlers who battle other teams of wrestlers; usually only one wrestler from each team is allowed in the ring at a time and teammates switch places inside and outside the ring by "tagging" or hand-slapping one another

title (TYE-tuhl) the championship

Triple Threat Match (TRIP-uhl THRET MACH) a wrestling match in which three wrestlers battle each other

World Heavyweight Champion (WURLD HEV-ee-wate CHAM-pee-uhn) a wrestler who holds one of the WWE's most important titles

WWE (DUHB-uhl-yoo DUHB-uhl-yoo EE) the main pro wrestling organization in the United States

WWE Championship (DUHB-uhl-yoo DUHB-uhl-yoo EE CHAM-pee-uhn-*ship*) one of the WWE's most important titles, along with the World Heavyweight Championship

Bibliography

"Randy Orton: The Evolution of a Predator" Vivendi (2011).

Men's Fitness Magazine

randy-orton.com

WWE.com

Read More

Nemeth, Jason D. *Randy Orton*. Mankato, MN: Capstone (2010).

Stone, Adam. *Randy Orton*. Minneapolis, MN: Bellwether Media (2012).

West, Tracy. *Cena and Orton: Rivalry in the Ring*. New York: Grosset & Dunlap (2011).

Learn More Online

To learn more about Randy Orton, visit
www.bearportpublishing.com/WrestlingsToughGuys

Index